HELPLINE
TEEN ISSUES AND ANSWERS ™

CYBERBULLYING
ONLINE SAFETY

TRACY BROWN

ROSEN
PUBLISHING®

New York

Published in 2014 by The Rosen Publishing Group, Inc.
29 East 21st Street, New York, NY 10010

Library of Congress Cataloging-in-Publication Data

Brown, Tracy.
Cyberbullying: online safety/Tracy Brown.—First edition.
    pages cm.—(Helpline: teen issues and answers)
Includes bibliographical references and index.
ISBN 978-1-4488-9450-5 (library binding)
1. Cyberbullying—Juvenile literature. 2. Cyberbullying—Prevention—Juvenile literature. 3. Internet and teenagers—Juvenile literature. I. Title.
HV6773.15.C92B76 2013
302.34'302854678—dc23

2012040917

Manufactured in the United States of America

CPSIA Compliance Information: Batch #S13YA: For further information, contact Rosen Publishing, New York, New York, at 1-800-237-9932.

CONTENTS

Internet and mobile phone technologies have had a massive effect on how people live, including how they work, shop, share, and learn. These technologies are tools that allow people to do the everyday things they've always done in faster, easier ways.

For the most part, the impact of these tools has been good, making life more convenient, improving global communication, and enabling easier access to information worldwide. But these technologies have also had more sinister effects, exposing individuals and businesses to hackers, computer viruses, identify theft, and cybercriminals.

Cyberbullying is a relatively new phenomenon made possible by the Internet and mobile phones. With access to a mobile telephone, a person can send a text message, take a photograph, record a video, and access the Internet. Social networking sites such as Facebook and Twitter are enormously popular means for sharing images and ideas, and unfortunately, not everything everyone has to say is kind.

Bullying is not new, but new technologies have made it easier for bullies to aggravate their victims twenty-four hours a day and with a far broader audience. Before the Internet, if a person was bullied at school, it was still a terrible experience—but at least it lasted only during the school hours. Now it's much harder to escape. Text messages and

Mobile phone and Internet technology are amazing tools that enable us to do everything easily—and that includes falling prey to a bully in cyberspace.

e-mails with hurtful content and social networking sites and blogs that attack and make fun of individuals are just some of the ways a cyberbully can humiliate or intimidate his or her victim.

There are ways to help prevent this practice. We will look at ways you can better protect yourself from cyberbullies, what behaviors count as bullying, and

what the law says about them. We will also talk about the impact cyberbullying has on a person's self-esteem and health, as well as the school and community atmosphere.

The Internet is a wonderful invention that everyone should be able to use and enjoy. Nobody deserves to be bullied, online or off. Everyone should do his or her part in ending cyberbullying, and the information contained here will give you information to help people do just that.

Bullies in Cyberspace

Have you ever known someone who seemed to enjoy being mean to other people, making them feel embarrassed or unliked, or even intimidated and scared? Have you ever had someone be mean to you in those ways, perhaps even someone who used to be your friend? Have you ever treated a person that way yourself?

A bully is a person who regularly and intentionally threatens, humiliates, or otherwise abuses a person. The victim is usually seen as different in some way—maybe he or she is smaller, less athletic, or quick to become upset by the bullying by crying or trying to fight back.

Bullies often get away with acting this way because people are afraid of them. Nobody wants to be the target, so nobody wants to stand up to a bully. In fact, many times other children will join in with the bully against their victim.

Social networking sites such as Twitter have connected the world in many ways, but they've also shown that words really can hurt you—even when users are limited to just 140 characters.

just so they don't become a victim themselves. It keeps the cycle going and makes the person being bullied feel even more alone.

Unfortunately, bullies have been around since the beginning of time. Common methods of bullying include actual physical attacks, such as hitting and kicking, and also teasing, making someone feel excluded or left out, and harassing by constantly picking on or pestering.

But technology has made a new form of bullying possible: cyberbullying. This section will look at what exactly cyberbullying is, what behaviors are considered cyberbullying, and why this form of peer abuse is so common.

WHAT IS CYBERBULLYING?

Cyberbullying means using technology to attack people, frighten them, make fun of them, embarrass them—the same things a regular bully likes to do, but online. Cyberbullying is a term used specifically for such technology-based harassment when a child, preteen, or teen is targeted by another child, preteen, or teen. (If an adult is involved, then it is called cyberharassment or cyberstalking, and that can be illegal.)

Cyberbullies engage in many different activities to harm their victims. They send threatening or insulting text messages. They harass their targets with voice mails, messages on social networking sites like Facebook, and in some cases fake Facebook profiles using their victim's name and image. Some cyberbullies create blogs to post untrue or unkind content—images and text—about their target. Cyberbullies are limited only by their imagination and understanding of technology.

If you have been bullied by someone online, or have been a bully yourself, you are not alone. According to a November 2010 government report, 4 percent of students ages twelve to eighteen were cyberbullied in 2007. In another study, conducted by the University of Toronto,

about half (49.5 percent) of middle and high school students asked said they had been bullied online, and 33.7 percent indicated they had bullied others online.

METHODS OF CYBERBULLYING

Cyberbullies take advantage of technologies that are meant to be enjoyed by friends and turn them into torture tools for their victims. And as technology continues to improve and evolve, bullies will likely find new ways to aggravate and abuse. So what counts as cyberbullying? How do you know when you are being targeted, or how can you tell if you have perhaps gone too far and bullied someone?

Harassment is one form of cyberbullying in which a bully is constantly sending a person cruel or threatening text messages or leaving equally harmful voice mails. Another form of cyberbullying is called denigration. This is another word for putting someone down, or attacking the person's character. This can be done in many ways, including posting lies about a person to a broad audience or altering photos of the person and distributing them.

Sometimes cyberbullies go so far as to pretend to be their victim. This is called impersonation, and it can be done by setting up a fake Twitter account or Facebook page and posting messages as if you are someone else or otherwise using someone else's online identify to leave comments or make remarks.

Interview with My Bully

The online magazine Salon.com ran an essay series in 2012 in which adults interviewed the bullies of their youth. Salon's editors hope the series will help bring closure to victims of bullying and perhaps even help build common ground between the bullied and the bully.

In her contribution to the series, author Mary Myung-Ok Lee, who suffered race-based bullying in high school, explained what happened when she spoke to her middle school bully. Her tormentor had teased Lee for being one of the few Asians in their Minnesota school in the 1970s. Although the impact of the teasing stayed with Lee—she admits to disliking herself for some years for her Asian background—her bully said she didn't remember teasing her. If she had, she said, she was just being a stupid preteen.

Although it's true that bullying is stupid, that doesn't make it harmless. The things we say because we are insecure, or think we are funny, or think other people will like us for them can do life-long damage to others.

Outing and tricking are terms for when a cyberbully shares something embarrassing or deeply personal about the victim online or via text messages with the intent of humiliating that person.

Cyberstalking takes things a little farther than cyberbullying. It means a person is constantly receiving messages that seem dangerous or threatening. These go beyond painful and less life-threatening humiliations and

Don't Mess with the Bus Lady

Although technology has opened the gates for new methods of merciless bullying, it can also be used for good. In June 2012, sixty-eight-year-old Karen Klein was riding a school bus in Greece, New York. She was a widow who worked as a bus monitor in her school district. As she sat on the bus one afternoon, she was put through a lengthy and brutal serving of verbal abuse by a group of

Karen Klein's experience with bullies and the outpour of generosity and love that the public showed her inspired her to start the Karen Klein Anti-Bullying Foundation.

kids. They told her she was fat, they made fun of her for being poor, and they said she was so ugly that her kids should kill themselves (in fact, her son had taken his own life, ten years before).

The incident was videotaped on the telephone of one of the abusers. The video, which plays for more than ten minutes, is very difficult to watch. Klein at first tries to ignore her aggressors, but as their insults continue and intensify, she eventually begins to cry. The video was leaked on the Internet and went viral. The outrage felt nationally when the video was shared shows that there is still humanity in the world, in spite of how mean some people can be. Thousands of people who don't even know the bus monitor raised more than $700,000 for her, and she was given a free trip for ten people to Disneyworld. Although the wrong was not righted, because of the Internet, Ms. Klein was able to feel the support of thousands of strangers.

irritations, and may be illegal, depending on the nature of the threat.

All of these methods use technology to abuse another person. They are all considered cyberbullying and have been shown to inflict great harm on bully victims.

CYBERBULLYING VERSUS TRADITIONAL BULLYING

Bullies have the same intentions online and off—to make another person feel bad about him- or herself. The terrible impact on health and self-esteem are the same for all forms of bullying. So why is cyberbullying getting so much attention? Bullies have always been around. Isn't cyber-bullying just more of the same?

Yes and no. Bullying is serious and wrong no matter what form it takes. People who do it are weak and mean. People who suffer it can be put through a lot of needless pain. But cyberbullying differs from more traditional offline or physical bullying in many ways. For one, the victim of the abuse can't avoid the bully simply by being physically away from him or her. Cyberbullying can occur anytime, no matter how far apart the bully is from the target. Any time a phone or computer is within reach, the bully can reach his or her victim.

Bullies are by nature cowards—picking on people they think are weaker to make themselves feel stronger. But online, they can be even more cowardly by keeping their identities a secret. It's easy to pretend to be someone else online. You can bully someone by creating an e-mail address or messaging account with a made-up name or by inventing a secret identity in a chat room. An anony-mous bully can be crueler, because he or she is not restricted by any social pressure.

Another way that cyberbullying is different from physi-cal bullying is the lack of supervision. When you are at school, your teachers and other students are around to watch what's going on. Although bullying still goes on, there is more of a chance that someone will try to stop a child from being bullied if it happens in person.

On a computer, there is less parental or other adult supervision. And bystanders on the Internet—often called lurkers—often don't feel the same responsibility to defend someone being bullied online. If you are watching something in person, it is harder to walk away from it. If you are just reading words in a chat room—no matter how insulting or mean they may be—it's easier to just ignore it or leave the site.

Finally, cyberbullies have a very broad audience. A spoken insult is heard only by people who are present when it occurs. But online, hurtful content can reach an endless number of people, causing more damage and humiliation to the victim.

10 Great Questions
TO ASK A CYBERBULLY

 **1** Why do you think you have a right to make someone else feel bad?

 2 In what ways does bullying someone else online make you feel better about yourself? In what ways does it make you feel bad?

 3 How would you feel if someone was harassing you online or via telephone?

 **4** If you don't like someone, can't you just ignore that person?

 **5** Do you think about how you are making people feel when you bully them?

 6 How do you think your parents would react if they knew how you treated others online?

 7 Do you or do you think you ever will regret causing pain to someone else?

 8 Where do you draw the line between harmless teasing and bullying?

 **9** At what point do you think your behavior should be punishable at school? By the law?

 **10** Do you think bullying someone else makes you someone your peers should like or admire?

Profile of a Bully

When you see someone treat someone else badly on a regular basis, it's easy to assume he or she is just a mean or bad person. But in truth, most people are not "bad" at the core. Sometimes people make things hard for others because they don't feel so good about themselves. Sometimes bullies are actually jealous of their victims or feel threatened by them. Sometimes people are just insecure and need to feel stronger or more accepted than someone else.

There are reasons why some people bully others. That does not mean there is an excuse for the behavior, but studies have shown that people who are bullies share some common characteristics. You don't have to start feeling sorry for bullies in your school, but understanding how they are feeling might help you take it less personally if you are bullied. It might also help you understand yourself better and change your behavior if you are someone

This section looks at some common traits of bullies, according to research. It also looks at why bullies do what they do. Because not all bullying is the same—some forms are more severe than others—the section also examines different types of bullying and different degrees of bullying.

COMMON TRAITS OF A BULLY

Everyone has it in them to be mean sometimes. You can have days where you feel disappointed or frustrated and take it out on someone else. Sometimes that person is your friend, sometimes a total stranger. But bullying is something else. Bullying means repeatedly attacking someone without cause because it makes you feel stronger or better. What kind of person would do that?

Although anyone can become a bully, there are some common traits that researchers have discovered that many bullies have in common. In a study of 558 sixth to eighth graders conducted by the Center for Adolescent Studies at Indiana University, it was concluded that bullies compare with nonbullies in the following ways:

- They watch more television.
- They misbehave more frequently at home.
- They spend less time at home with adults.
- When they are disciplined at home, they face more forceful punishments.
- They have fewer positive adult role models.

It can be hard to feel sympathy for someone who is making your life difficult, but it's important to recognize that bullies may act that way because they are hurting, too.

Bullies' Regrets

When you're a kid you don't always think about the long-term consequences of the things you do or how you might feel about things later. Regret is a terrible feeling. You don't get to go back in time and make different choices. A person who is bullied may carry the scars for years to come, but the bully may also feel the burden of his or her actions well into adulthood.

Kevin A. Hansen compiled the regrets of adults who had bullied other children in their youth for a June 2012 piece for the *Huffington Post*. These stories were originally shared on the confessional site, Secret Regrets. Here are two examples:

• I was pretty consistently bullied from nursery school on. When I was in 7th grade, (trying, I suppose to be one of the crowd) I threw a note at a pudgy, dirty, smelly girl who was avoided by everyone. The note read, "You stink." As it rolled across the lunch table, I was appalled at what I'd done. She read it with no change of expression. I never got up the courage to apologize. Several years later, she committed suicide, and it came out that she had been kept in awful conditions and been regularly beaten and sexually abused. I'll be 62 pretty soon, and I still think of her and how I added to her misery. Before that day, I'd always been one to stick up for the underdog, and I've been trying to make up for that one evil act ever since.

• I regret not helping a girl who was being bullied, which I guess makes me a bully myself. Last year during school, I witnessed her get bullied to the point of sobbing, screaming, and throwing things at the tormentors outside. The teachers had to have heard or seen it happening, but they did nothing, and neither did anyone else. They just watched it go down. I had wanted to be her friend for a while, and I knew she had been bullied a lot before. I will always regret not trying to stop them, or not trying to comfort her. I can't imagine having something like that happening to me with so many people watching, only to have them do nothing. I'm so sorry.

- They have fewer positive peer influences or friends.
- They get into more fights.

While the behavior is unacceptable, it makes sense that if you do not grow up seeing adults be friends with each other and deal with disappointment or disagreement in healthy, positive ways, you will not learn how to handle these things yourself. If punishments are forceful or even violent—if your parents yell or even hit you—then you may learn to "punish" people for wronging you in similar ways. And you will probably feel pretty angry and want to take it out on someone.

Think about your family life. Are the adults in your home calm and respectful to each other? Are they there for you when you need them? Positive role models are key to learning how to treat people fairly while being treated fairly in return. Not everyone has such good examples, and sometimes that can make a person a bully.

HIGH-SCALE BULLIES

Not all forms of bullying are the same. Although they are both wrong, there is a difference between someone who teases another person on occasion and someone who regularly threatens that person with physical harm.

The researchers in the Indiana University study mentioned in the previous section identified children who were "high-scale bullies." These are bullies who engage in behaviors that go beyond tormenting to actually hurting and humiliating others in more extreme ways.

The study found the following to be true of high-scale bullies:

1. Thirty-six percent of them came from single-parent homes.
2. Another thirty-two percent had stepparents.
3. They had easier access to guns.
4. They had more exposure to gang activities.

Not everyone who grows up in these environments becomes a violent bully. But there are factors that can contribute to whether someone is likely to be a bully. It is good for society to identify these factors so they can be addressed.

GIRL VERSUS BOY BULLIES

When you think of a bully, do you think of a boy or a girl? If your definition is only someone who beats up smaller kids on the playground, then you might think only boys are bullies. (Although it is true that boys tend to be more so, girls can also be violent, and in fact violence in girls is on the rise.)

Girls can also be bullies, but studies show that girls usually bully in ways different from their boy counterparts. Girls tend to be nonviolent and prefer to bully by spreading false rumors to hurt another girl's reputation. They can randomly decide to be friends or to exclude.

Girls are competitive in different ways than boys. (Again, this is broadly speaking—there are always

It's Not Just the Kids

You may sometimes wonder what a bully's parents would think if they knew how their children acted toward others. Unfortunately, sometimes the children are not the only ones to blame: parents have also been found guilty of bullying children. In 2010, Jennifer Petkov, a thirty-three-year-old woman, began cyberbullying a seven-year-old neighbor who was dying of Huntington's disease.

In 2006, thirteen-year-old Megan Meier developed a relationship on Myspace with an individual whom she thought was a new boy in the area. In fact, she was communicating with Lori Drew, the mother of a friend of hers, who was pretending to be a sixteen-year-old boy. When the boy told Meier, who suffered from depression, that everybody hated her and the world would be a better place without her, Meier committed suicide.

When an adult bullies a child, it is no longer called cyberbullying, but cyberharassment. This is punishable by law. In the case of Jennifer Petkov, the grandmother of the dying girl was able to get a restraining order. In the case of Lori Drew, the court ruled that they could not prove a direct link to the girl's death, but Drew was charged with a computer fraud misdemeanor.

Lori Drew leaving a federal courthouse in Los Angeles, July 2, 2009. Unfortunately, many kids who bully are mimicking the behavior of their parents.

exceptions!) Boys may compete physically in sports, whereas girls sometimes compete for popularity. This can make it very tempting for girls to want to ruin another girl's chance of popularity or acceptance among their peers.

Because of the quiet nature in which girls bully, it can be difficult for a teacher to detect or know who the girl bully is. If you see a group of girls standing in a corner at school, you might think they are just friends talking

You may think of boys being the ones getting into physical fights, but girls can be much worse to each other through less obvious, more psychological means that leave lasting emotional scars.

between classes. But in fact, it could be a gang of girls telling an unsuspecting girl that she is no longer welcome in their group, or something equally hurtful. Girls tend to bully in packs, with one ringleader who intimidates the others to follow along. Girls who don't want to risk their own social status are afraid to stand up to the bully, and that can add to the bully's power.

Because of the nonphysical ways that girls tend to bully, cyberbullying methods are increasingly used by girls who want to make another girl's life miserable. The Internet makes it possible to destroy someone's reputation by spreading lies about that person on a massive scale. What used to be graffiti on a bathroom wall can now be spread to countless people on a Facebook wall.

WHY THEY DO IT

When you watch a kid mistreat another, you probably wonder why he or she is acting that way. There are as many reasons why a person bullies another as there are ways to bully someone. Perhaps the bully is deeply frustrated, either with home or school, and can't communicate these feelings other than to be cruel to someone else. Some kids who bully may actually have clinical behavioral or personality disorders that have not been addressed.

Most often, bullies act the way they do because they want to fit in. Sometimes they feel insecure and worry that others will not like them or accept them. Peer acceptability is very important to young people. If a preteen or teen worries that he or she may be excluded, sometimes they

The only way to end the practice of bullying is to learn to become more tolerant of each other and encourage everyone to feel good about who they are.

will find another child to bully to show the "cool" kids that they have someone beneath them.

A study in the United Kingdom found that what is valued by a school or community can predict which kids may be bullied. Who are the popular kids at your school, and what activities do they engage in? Are they athletic? Do they dress in expensive clothes? Do you live in a very conservative town that frowns on homosexuality? On people who dress differently? On people who have emigrated from another country or follow a different faith than the majority?

It is likely that the kids who do not blend in with the presumed "right" way to be will be the victims of bullies. This will only go away when people learn to accept people for who they are and to admire people because they are good people, not because they are good-looking or good athletes.

Remember, just because there may be a reason for a behavior, it does not make the behavior excusable. We are all responsible for handling ourselves and our emotions. We have to address the issues that make us angry, the things that we are tempted to take out on someone else. If a child is mistreated at home, he or she should tell someone and get out of the situation rather than beat up another child. If you feel insecure about your abilities, you have to deal with those feelings rather than make someone else feel bad, too.

CHAPTER 3

How to Protect Yourself from a Cyberbully

How do you think it feels to have someone bully you online or via mobile phone? Imagine if you were receiving a constant stream of vicious text or voice mail messages, perhaps from someone who doesn't identify him- or herself. Or imagine turning on your computer at night to find other kids from your class spreading lies or making fun of you on a social networking site. It's not physical pain that it causes, but it's a real hurt that nobody should have to suffer.

The number one thing to understand about bullying is that it is about the bully, not the victim. Bullying isn't personal. That may sound crazy, as of course it feels very personal when you are picked out to be bullied. Bullies hone in on your perceived weak spots, on the things you are sensitive to, and exploit them publicly, online or off. But bullying is more about the bully needing attention

The best way to protect yourself from cyberbullying is to exercise good judgment when giving anyone access to you, be it via your telephone number or your e-mail address or social networking sites.

more about the bully needing acceptance. Often bullying escalates because the kids doing the harm begin to compete with each other to see who can get the biggest laugh. The person who is the focus of the attack really isn't the point.

In no way is it the fault of the victim of bullying when he or she is put through any kind of abuse. But understanding what a bully looks for in a potential victim may help you avoid suffering at the hands of a bully. Further, knowing what you can do if you are being bullied can help you put an end to the situation. Let's look at how to avoid and how to react to bullying.

COMMON TRAITS OF BULLYING VICTIMS

It is worth repeating: if you are being bullied, it is not your fault. Nobody deserves to be treated that way. A bully is someone who needs to pick on someone for his or her own personal gain—to build his or her self-esteem or to preserve social standing. Who suffers at the hand of the bully, unfortunately, is mostly up to the bully. So what qualities does a bully look for in a potential victim?

Studies show that bullies most frequently torment quieter kids, perhaps kids who don't have a lot of friends. If a person is quiet, the bully will assume he or she will not stand up for him- or herself. If a person doesn't seem to have a strong circle of friends, the bully will think there is nobody who will stand up for him or her. Being quiet or not being all that social are not reasons why you

If You Can't Prevent It, Report It!

If you are bullied, you need to let the right people know. Sites like Facebook have codes of behavior that protect against bullying. Fake profiles are not allowed and are taken down if reported. Users are banned for posting content that is offensive, pornographic, or violent.

Twitter does not automatically remove offensive content and encourages users to ignore content they find offensive. However, if you are being personally threatened or your private information is being exposed, you can submit what is called a support ticket via Twitter's help center. You can report if someone is posting private information, stealing your tweets, posting offensive content, sending abusive messages, or sending violent threats.

You can and should also report cyberbullying incidents to your teachers, parents, or any other trusted adult. Cyberbullying should not be taken any less seriously than more traditional forms, and schools and parents need to be responsible for seeing that children are protected both online and off.

should suffer at the hands of a bully, of course, but bullies are weak and go after who they perceive to be the easiest targets.

Bullies also get satisfaction from being able to see that they are getting to their victims. They want to know that the person they are attacking is suffering. This is the really cruel part of bullying and the most upsetting. If you see someone crying, how do you feel? Do you feel sad for him or her? Do you want to help? Most people see someone upset and want to help. A bully sees the person they are tormenting cry and feels victorious. It's hard to imagine being so mean and even harder to imagine that bullies do it to be liked or to like themselves better.

Bullies pick on kids who cry easily, who try to fight back but can't, either because they are physically not capable or because they are not as quick with insults. Not that being good at making people feel bad is a good thing, but bullies look for anything to make fun of, and if someone tries to fight back and isn't good at it, the bully will just get more joy out of it.

Kids with certain social abilities, like a good sense of humor, are better able to avoid being bullied. If you are able to laugh off an insult at the beginning, the situation will be less likely to escalate into full-fledged bullying. The more you react, the more the bully will enjoy bullying you, and the longer it'll last and the worse it'll get. If you don't give your bully the satisfaction of fear, sadness, or failed attempts at retaliation, he or she will often move on.

KNOW WHO YOUR FRIENDS ARE

Bullies are in a position of perceived power. Perhaps a star football player in your school likes to pick on the

Social networking and talking on the phone are supposed to be fun activities, and they are, if you do them only with people who like you and make you feel good about yourself.

smaller-framed boys in your class, the nonathletic kids who are probably very talented in other, less popular things. Or maybe the most popular girl in your class likes to make life miserable for other girls who may be less pretty or have less expensive clothes. In many schools, people look up to the bullies because the bullies represent the perfect social position. They seem to be who everyone wants to be, and the farther you are from that ideal, the less popular you are.

All of this is normal. It happens in every school, and it has happened for generations. You're at an age where social standing feels enormously important. What you may not realize is that when school is behind you and you head off to college or your first job, the social "ideal" will change as your environment changes. It may be more important to be smart than pretty. It may be more important to be sensitive to others than to be athletic. But in middle and high school, it can be hard not to want to be in with the in crowd.

And that's one way many people become the victims of bullies. They want to be the bully's friend. They look up to him or her and want the bully's approval. This gives the person enormous power over you. If you will do anything to make that person think you are cool, then you are allowing yourself to be a victim. If you keep going back for more, you will keep getting more, and probably it will get worse each time.

It is so important to know who your real friends are. Surround yourself with people who like you for the qualities you possess, for the shared interests you have, for the way you support and help each other. Wherever you attend school and whatever you're like, there is someone who will be a true friend to you. Find that person, and don't chase after people who seem to be what you "ought" to be. You don't have to be anything but yourself.

PROTECT YOURSELF ONLINE

Know who your friends are online as well as off. If a person isn't kind to you, or if you just really don't know him or her all that well, do not feel you have to "friend" the person on Facebook. Facebook has created a whole new obsession in people to collect as many friends as they can. The number of friends you have on the site has become an indicator of popularity, when in fact it is quite meaningless. What you share on your Facebook timeline is very personal. Every comment you make, every photo you post, and every status update can be seen by every one of your contacts. Make sure you want each of your friends to be privy to this information. Keep in mind also that everyone you are friends with can see what other people post on your wall. You may not want your aunt in Wisconsin to read a dirty joke posted by some jerk in your class and think it represents you. So be careful who you friend.

Equally, do not share other personal "cyber" details with people you don't know and trust. Don't be flattered if someone you admire from afar asks for this information. If you don't know that they can be trusted, keep it to yourself. Do not give anyone your phone number or e-mail address or tell him or her what name you use online. Certainly do not give out your account passwords.

If a person doesn't have this information, he or she has less chance to harass you online. Of course it's easy

Making It Cool to Be Kind

Although it's easy to say, "Tell a teacher" to someone who is being bullied, the reality in many cases is victims will be very hesitant to do so. Many kids who suffer at the hands of a bully (virtually or otherwise) fear reporting it will only make things worse.

Angus Watson is an adult living in the UK. He told the *Telegraph* that he used to be a bully in his schooldays and that the odd bit of teasing is very normal for kids. Determining where you fall on a perceived social ladder is, sometimes unfortunately, a big part of being a preteen or teen. Watson says he stopped bullying when he was trying to impress a girl by picking on a kid smaller than he was. She was not charmed by his meanness, and he soon stopped. Rather than encourage victims to report the bullying, Watson says, antibullying campaigns should be stressing to bullies that what they are doing is not cool.

In an ideal world, bullies would realize the error of their ways and stop being cruel to other people. However, as long as bullies continue to pester, targets of bullies should protect themselves. Although it's not the easiest path to take, reporting abuse is the way to go. Your school and the parents in your community can't address a problem that you keep secret. And when it comes to online bullying, get yourself out of the situation by defriending, blocking, leaving chat rooms, and so on. Know and exercise your options.

to get this information from others, so be very careful to whom you reveal any of it. It won't prevent all forms of cyberbullying, but it will reduce the ways your bully can access you.

PRIVACY SETTINGS ON FACEBOOK

If you do friend someone on Facebook and he or she abuses the privilege, you can unfriend or unsubscribe his or her profile or even block the person from your account. Unfriending means you are no longer linked on Facebook and cannot access each others' timelines, other than to see the basic information you allow the public to see. Unsubscribing means you will see fewer updates from that person in your news feed.

Blocking is more severe than unfriending. You can block someone entirely using the privacy settings. This means he or she can't send you messages through Facebook or access your timeline. You will not see posts he or she makes anywhere on Facebook. You are both still users of Facebook, but you will never see his or her activity and vice versa.

You can also do a lot more to customize your privacy settings in Facebook. You can create groups, separating close friends from acquaintances, for example, and choose for only certain groups to be able to see certain posts on your timeline. You can set it so nobody can post on your timeline, or you can customize things more specifically. You can determine who can post on your timeline, who can see what others post there, and who can see

Cyberspace is an extension of real life, as on Facebook. Only connect online with people who respect you off-line. If someone mistreats you in person, keep them out of your cyber-life.

u connect

life.

posts you've been tagged in on your timeline.

The Facebook privacy settings change frequently, so pay attention to what changes are made and make sure you are in control of who has access to your content. Review your current settings and customize them as you wish by clicking the downward facing arrow on the top right corner of you Facebook page and clicking "Privacy Settings."

PRIVACY ON MSN MESSENGER

On MSN Messenger, you can block a contact by clicking "Block" in the tool-bar in a conversation or in the main window and right-clicking the person's name and clicking "Block." Simply deleting a contact does not block that person from contacting you.

You can see who is monitoring your status by clicking "Tools > Options > Privacy" and looking at your My Allow List. If you don't recognize some-one, confirm their identify by sending them a message before adding them to your contacts. Never add someone you don't know.

Before you share anything on Twitter, remember how many people can access it and think about how it will make them feel—you don't want to become a bully yourself.

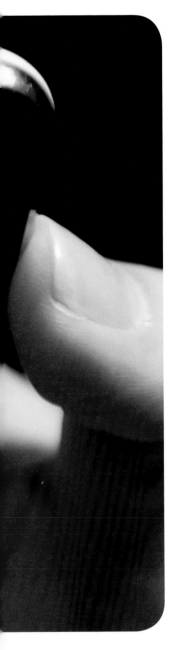

PRIVACY ON TWITTER

Although it may seem like the intention of Twitter is to have as many followers as possible, if someone is crossing the line and bullying you, or if you just want to protect yourself from strangers or people you know abusing you online, you can block followers from seeing your tweets and you can adjust your privacy settings so that only followers you have approved can read and respond to your tweets. Check the privacy settings to see your options. And keep in mind that privacy settings change often on Web sites, so check each individual site for updates.

The Impact of Cyberbullying

CHAPTER 4

The old adage that "sticks and stones may break my bones, but names will never hurt me" no longer holds true. Cyberbullying may not be physical, but it still leaves scars. Not just on the victims but also on the bullies themselves and on the community in which the bullying takes place.

Bullies have always been around, but technology has made it easier to bully around the clock, in much sneakier and sometimes even anonymous ways. Because a bully can hide behind a false online identity, kids who may not have had it in them to bully someone in person are finding ways to aggravate their targets in more sinister, cowardly ways. This increases the instance of bullying.

Researchers have been looking into what impact this increased and more technically sophisticated form of bullying has on society. In this section, we'll look at some of

What may seem like just a joke or harmless fun can actually cause lifelong torment to the victim of a bully. Hurting someone is never innocent, no matter what form it takes.

the findings of this research. Cyberbullying is relatively new and is often unnoticed by parents and teachers—many of whom are not as comfortable with technology as the kids

Two students help another to a bus after the 1999 Columbine High School shootings, in which two students, who experts suspected were bullied, killed twelve students and one teacher before taking their own lives.

they raise and teach—and it is important that everyone recognize its seriousness and potential for real harm.

EFFECTS ON SCHOOL CLIMATE AND COMMUNITY

Community climate and attitude and bullying are closely connected. For example, if you live in a town where most people are one way—either the same race, the same religion, or the same sexual orientation—a "norm" can be established that makes anyone who is different from the others or doesn't fit in a potential victim of bullying.

Bullying can be the result of a community attitude, but it can also be the cause of problems and negative effects in a community, be it your town or school. In a community where bullying is commonplace, there's an environment of exclusion. Some people are always left out. They are not welcome in certain places and not included in parties or other celebrations. If the bullying is particularly bad, people may be afraid to walk the halls or be alone in a place where they are more vulnerable. This impacts not just those being bullied or doing the bullying but everyone who is part of the community.

Cyberbullying can also affect academic performance in school. In some cases, students avoid going to school because they are being cyberbullied, which makes their grades suffer and brings down the performance of the

"It Gets Better"

The "It Gets Better" campaign is an Internet-based initiative working for the prevention of teen suicide as a result of bullying. Dan Savage and his husband, Terry Miller, launched the project in 2010 to help prevent in particular the suicides of gay, lesbian, and transgender teens who were victimized because of their sexuality.

On the project's Web site, gay, lesbian, and transgender adults post videos addressing kids and helping convey the message that if kids can just get through the bumpy ride of adolescence, life will indeed get better. In the first week, more than two hundred videos were posted. Today, the site has more than thirty thousand entries and has had more than forty million visitors. A book of essays from the project was published in 2011.

school. High rates of cyberbullying mean many students are spending an abundance of time on smartphones or computers in school hours, which takes their attention away from classwork and lowers their performance in school.

Cyberbullying—and all forms of bullying—can also have more violent impacts on a school or community. Bullying victims have been shown to be more likely to fight back with violent measures. In a study of fifteen school shootings in the United States in the 1990s, the shooters were victims of bullies in twelve of them. Of course, these are extreme cases, but in an environment that allows or even encourages the victimization of some community members, things can escalate to tragic levels.

EFFECTS ON VICTIMS' HEALTH

Being bullied can have terrible consequences for the mental health of victims. Depression and anxiety are common effects of cyberbullying and can be particularly difficult to identify given the more subtle nature of cyber versus more traditional bullying. Dr. Niranjan Karnik, a psychiatrist at the University of Chicago, makes a point of asking patients not only if they are bullied but if they are cyberbullied in particular. All mental health professionals are being encouraged to ask patients about the practice of cyberbullying to find out whether the patient is either a victim or a bully.

Being depressed is different from feeling sad. Of course it doesn't feel good to be insulted or teased, but a depressed person feels more than just momentarily down as a reaction to something unkind. Depressed people experience long bouts of hopelessness and despair. They can have uncontrollable crying episodes or find it extremely difficult to get out of bed. They often feel anxious, frightened, worthless, and irritable. A depressed

What About the Bully's Self-Esteem?

Although it's easy to blame the bully for any ill effects his or her behavior might have on his or her own life, most people who are bullies are not that happy or confident either. Very often a bully is also being bullied, either by someone bigger or more popular, or by a family member at home. Picking on someone else is an expression of insecurity. Bullies generally do not feel that good about themselves.

There is also evidence that people who bully others in their youth are less successful in life and have lower self-esteem than those who do not engage in bullying activity. A child who is a bully, for example, is more likely to do badly in or drop out of school. He or she is more likely to end up in prison. Bullies are more likely to have lifelong difficulty in developing healthy relationships with others, and they have increased odds at being involved in spousal or child abuse as an adult. If you have the urge or tendency to lash out at others, it's a good idea to figure out what is causing you to have those feelings so you can resolve the problem and avoid some of these pitfalls now and later in life.

person may dramatically change his or her sleeping or eating patterns or even have thoughts about suicide.

Depression and anxiety can lead to other physical conditions. For example, many people who suffer depression try to self-medicate with drugs and alcohol, leading to addictions that can destroy their health. Other people turn to food addictions or other eating disorders. Rates of sexual promiscuity and its negative effects—teenage pregnancy and the spread of sexually transmitted diseases—also increase with people who suffer from depression or anxiety.

Higher rates of depression are seen in both victims and perpetrators of more traditional forms of bullying. However, research conducted by the National Institutes of Health (NIH) shows that, in cases of cyberbullying, only the victims show an increased rate of depression. This is perhaps because the bully in cyberbullying cases does not have to confront his or her victim face to face, but can hide behind a telephone or computer screen, which reduces the stress he or she may feel during or after the bullying episode.

HOW BEING BULLIED AFFECTS YOUR SELF-ESTEEM

Self-esteem refers to the attitude a person has about him- or herself. A person's self-esteem is affected by many factors, but a big one is how society and the person's peers view him or her. If a person is mostly accepted by peers, is respected, and is included in social activities, then that person is likely to have higher self-esteem. On the flipside, if a person is frequently rejected, and made to feel excluded and isolated, he or she is likely to have lower self-esteem.

Having high self-esteem is integral to being successful socially and academically, but it also directly impacts your physical health. A person with low self-esteem is less likely to take good care of him- or herself, to treat his or her body with respect by eating well, to sleep enough, and to resist drugs and alcohol. He or she is more likely to be sexually promiscuous.

So, how does cyberbullying affect self-esteem? In research conducted by the Cyberbullying Research Center, in a group of approximately two thousand randomly selected middle school students, those kids who reported being victimized by cyberbullies had significantly lower self-esteem than those who reported no abuse. This is also true of cyberbullies—those who do the bullying also have lower self-esteem. This makes sense because a person who feels good about him- or herself doesn't feel the need to pick on other people.

Being alone or having just a few good friends is much better for your health and happiness than trying too hard to hang out with people who treat you badly.

People with low self-esteem are unlikely to simply outgrow the negative feelings they harbor about themselves. How your peers treat you and view you in your adolescence can unfortunately influence for the rest of your life how you see and behave toward yourself. Every preteen and teen has similar doubts and insecurities. How you deal with them can have a lasting effect on your life. If you choose to bully someone or if you are bullied, you will likely feel less good about yourself.

TRAGIC CONSEQUENCE: SUICIDE

The most horrific outcome of cyberbullying is the number of teen suicides that have been the direct result of bullying online. Depression, low self-esteem, fear, and isolation have driven many teens

A vigil is held at a high school in South Hadley, MA, in 2010, for Phoebe Prince, who committed suicide after being bullied. Two of her teenage tormenters pled guilty to charges of criminal harassment.

to end their lives. Some high-profile cases in recent years have brought the public's attention to the seriousness of cyberbullying and all forms of harassment.

In 2010, nine teenaged girls were indicted on charges including statutory rape (later dropped) and stalking after Phoebe Prince killed herself at just fifteen years old. Prince was the victim of unrelenting cyberbullying by fellow students. Prince had recently moved to America from Ireland, and as a new freshman in her high school began dating a senior football player. The girls who harassed her were likely jealous of her and wanted to put her in her place. They attacked her with an onslaught of text messages and Facebook posts, as well as picking on her at school. Teachers apparently witnessed this and did nothing.

There are too many similarly heartbreaking stories. Alexis Pilkington was a popular athlete who took her life at seventeen after being bullied online. Ryan Halligan was just thirteen years old when he ended his life, the victim of incessant taunting and harassment online and in person.

Suicide is the third-leading cause of death in teenagers. According to some research, 14 percent of young people have considered suicide at one point. Children who are victims of bullying are two to nine times more likely to have suicidal thoughts. There are some signs to look for in a person who may be considering suicide: a potentially suicidal person may give away possession that he or she cherishes. A suicidal person may talk about suicide, may hint that things would be better without him or her around, or frequently express an inability to deal with things any longer. These indicators should not be ignored. If anyone is showing any signs that he or she is depressed or suicidal, get that person help. The teen years are a particularly difficult and sensitive time. It's hard enough to deal with the pressures without adding to them by bullying each other and making each other feel worthless. Instead, build each other up and help each other out. It serves everyone in the end and might actually save lives.

MYTHS and FACTS

MYTH

Bullies do what they do because they are stronger and more confident than their victims.

FACT

Many bullies are deeply insecure and act out against others in order to feel more powerful. A person who bullies another has often been the victim of bullying and seeks out a perceived "weaker" target in order to improve his or her social standing.

MYTH

Victims of bullies are weak. If they were tougher, they wouldn't be bullied.

FACT

Anyone can be the victim of a bully. Bullies are motivated by many things: trying to bring down someone they think is "better" than them, reacting out of jealousy, wanting to appear cool in front of peers, or feeling empowered by making another person feel bad. The reasons for bullying all have to do with the bully and not the victim. Nobody deserves to be bullied.

MYTH

Cyberbullying isn't as serious as actual bullying because nobody really gets hurt.

FACT

Research shows that the effects of cyberbullying on victims are just as bad if not worse than traditional "in-person" bullying. It is harder to escape a cyberbully because a cyberbully can reach his or her victim twenty-four hours a day. Cyberbullies often act anonymously, so the victim doesn't know who the bully is.

Cyberbullying and the Law

Because cyberbullying is a relatively new problem, lawmakers are unsure how to handle it. Nobody deserves to be harassed, of course, and bullying is unethical and unkind—but that doesn't mean it's always illegal. Free speech means people are allowed to post messages on social networking sites or in chat rooms that may make people angry or feel hurt.

From a legal standpoint, it's not always clear where to draw the line between a person using his or her mobile phone to swap gossip—perhaps not nice, but not always intended to harm—and a person using the same device to aggravate a target mercilessly.

Different states have different laws about cyberbullying and bullying in general, and there is no federal law against cyberbullying. Some people who have been the victim of a cyberbully, or in some cases the parents or

The problem of cyberbullying has captured so much attention worldwide, largely through stories of victims' suicides, that lawmakers are now looking into new ways to protect people from being abused online.

guardians of a victim, have attempted to sue or have prosecuted the bully. These cases are helping bring national attention to the problem, which may lead to the passing of more laws to protect those victimized by a cyberbully.

CAN YOU SUE YOUR BULLY?

In May 2012, a thirteen-year-old girl in Georgia decided to sue two classmates and their parents over a fake Facebook page the classmates had created that depicted her as a marijuana smoker, included doctored photos of her that were unflattering, and indicated she was racist and sexually active.

The girl, Alex Boston, sued her bullies for libel— the practice of publishing information known to be false that can damage a person's reputation. The parents of the accused were named in the case because they paid

Alex Boston, fourteen, checks her e-mail on her cell phone at home in Acworth, Georgia, in 2012. Awaiting the results of her libel lawsuit against cyberbullies, she is once again online in peace.

for the Internet access. Boston and her lawyer decided to sue for libel because they felt they had no other recourse.

Boston had reported the abuse to school officials who said there was nothing they could do because the bullying took place off campus. Although Georgia has laws allowing schools to punish students who bully other students on campus, these laws do not include bullying via telephone or computer. Because cyberbullying does not occur in a specific place, it's unclear who is responsible for punishing or policing cyberbullies.

Boston's case will likely set the precedent for other anti-cyberbullying lawsuits. It shows that if suing for cyberbullying isn't an option, you have other choices. There are laws against defamation (damaging one's character by publishing false statements). There are laws that protect an individual's privacy, and violations of privacy include publishing or distributing information that is personal or private, as well as representing someone publicly in a way that would be offensive to most people.

Other Ways to Take Action Against Cyberbullying

Having laws to make cyberbullying punishable may help reduce the instances of online bullying. It could spare potential targets by discouraging would-be bullies from attacking, if only from fear of punishment. But without such laws in place, there are other ways you can take action to end cyberbullying.

STOP Cyberbullying is an organization dedicated to taking a stand against online abuse. Its founders urge children to fight cyberbullying by not participating in the practice and by not sitting back in silence when others are being harassed. STOP Cyberbullying would like all children to take the following pledge:

If I witness cyberbullying, I will not join in, nor will I stand by idly. I realize that bullies thrive on the support and attention of bystanders. I promise I will not support cyberbullies. I will stand up for what is right and report cyberbullying to the appropriate people.

I promise to be aware of what I say and do on line, how my actions impact others, and will not become a cyberbully.

I promise to use good "digital hygiene" by using strong passwords and not sharing them. I will regularly update and use good virus and malware protection. I will protect my computer from malicious code and hackers.

There are laws against causing a person severe emotional stress, and certainly there are laws against threats of physical harm. If cyberbullying goes so far as to cross these lines, it is possible to take legal action. Boston's case will be a strong indicator of how the courts will lean on these issues going forward.

STATE LAWS AGAINST CYBERBULLYING

To date, nineteen states have enacted some form of cyberbullying law, including Arkansas, California, Delaware, Florida, Idaho, Iowa, Kansas, Maryland, Minnesota, Missouri, Nebraska, New Jersey, North Carolina, Oklahoma, Oregon, Pennsylvania, Rhode Island, South Carolina, and Washington. In many cases, the laws permit schools to punish bullies with suspension if the bullying takes place on school grounds. In some states these laws are being expanded to include cyberbullying.

In Arkansas, a law was recently passed that allows school officials to take action against cyberbullies even if the bullying did not take place on school grounds. In Idaho, school officials can suspend students who bully or harass other students using a telephone or computer. Iowa requires schools to develop anti-cyberbullying policies that include bullying in schools, on school property, or at any school function or school-sponsored activity.

New Jersey has tough antibullying laws that now include bullying conducted by "electronic communication."

Schools have the power to punish cyberbullies even when the bullying takes place off campus. In Vermont, there is a $500 fine for cyberbullying.

There are laws against what is called cyberstalking in many states, but cyberbullying does not fit into that category. Cyberstalking means a person eighteen or older is bullying a minor. Right or wrong, many school administrators, parents, and legal professionals consider cyberbullying to be no more than normal adolescent behavior—just an ugly part of growing up, but not lawsuit-worthy. Check online for the latest information about state laws against cyberbullying.

FEDERAL LAWS AGAINST CYBERBULLYING

As of today, there is no federal law against cyberbullying. In 2009, the Megan Meier Cyberbullying Prevention Act was proposed. The bill is named after a girl who took her own life as a result of a Myspace cyberbullying incident involving the mother of a friend of hers.

The bill would make it against the law to "transmit in interstate or foreign commerce any communication, with the intent to coerce, intimidate, harass, or cause substantial emotional distress to a person, using electronic means to support severe, repeated, and hostile behavior."

The bill has not been passed. It may seem obvious that harassing anyone by any means is wrong and should therefore be punishable. But it's a cloudy area. Because the United States allows free speech to all of its citizens,

Mourning mother Tina Meier holds up photos of her daughter, Megan, who killed herself in October 2006, the victim of a Myspace hoax in which the mother of a friend, Lori Drew, was involved.

the government is very hesitant to pass laws that limit the expression of Americans. Laws need to be applicable in all cases and circumstances in order to be fair. Although picking on a twelve-year-old to the point where he or she no longer wants to live is something everyone should be against, could the law apply whenever anyone's feelings are hurt online? It's difficult to measure what is and what is not cyberbullyng from a legal point of view. Is it cyber-bullying only if it occurs over a long period of time, or can it be cyberbullying if it happens just once? What degree of bullying is considered illegal, and who decides? It's hard to know where to draw the line between protecting citizens and limiting their freedom of expression.

BULLY A person who regularly torments another person.

CHAT ROOM An online forum where people have discussions in real-time.

CYBERBULLY A person under eighteen who bullies someone using telephone and Internet technology.

CYBERSTALKER A person over eighteen who torments or bullies another person using telephone and Internet technology.

FACEBOOK A social media site where people post photos and messages.

HARASS To persistently torment or annoy.

LAWSUIT A case in a court of law.

LIBEL The act of publishing information known to be false that can damage a person's reputation.

PEER PRESSURE The social influence other people have on an individual.

PERPETRATOR A person who commits a crime or offense.

REGRET To feel sadness for past actions.

SELF-ESTEEM How a person views or thinks about him- or herself.

SOCIAL NETWORKING Connecting and communicating with others online.

SUICIDE The act of ending one's own life.

SUSPENSION A punishment in which a student is not allowed to come to school or do school work.

TARGET A person who is selected as a potential victim.

TEXT MESSAGE An electronic message sent in real time via telephone.

TWEET A message posted on Twitter.

TWITTER A social networking site in which people post messages of 140 characters or less.

UNETHICAL Lacking moral principles.

VICTIM A person against whom a crime or offense is committed.

FOR MORE INFORMATION

Bullying Canada
471 Smythe Street
P.O. BOX 27009
Fredericton, NB E3B 9M1
Canada
(877) 352-4497
Web site: http://www.bullyingcanada.ca
    /content/239639
This nonprofit, youth-created organization is dedicated
    to educating and advising on cyberbullying issues
    across Canada.

Cyber Bullying Prevention
5N426 Meadowview Lane
St. Charles, IL 60175
(847) 769-7495
Web site: http://www.cyberbullyingprevention.com
Cyber Bullying Prevention is dedicated to raising aware-
    ness of cyberbullying and its negative impacts.

Girls, Inc.
120 Wall Street
New York, NY 10005
212-509-2000
http://www.girlsinc.org
This organization inspires all girls to be strong, smart,
    and bold through life-changing programs and

experiences that help girls navigate gender, eco-
nomic, and social barriers.

The International Bullying Prevention Association
628 Albatross Lane
Brownsburg, IN 46112
615-983-6820
http://www.stopbullyingworld.org
This organization is dedicated to supporting research
into bullying and working toward prevention of
bullying.

It Gets Better
8023 Beverly Boulevard #191
Los Angeles, CA 90048
Web site: http://www.itgetsbetter.org
The It Gets Better Project was created to show young
LGBT people the levels of happiness, potential, and
positivity their lives will reach if they can just get
through their teen years.

StopBullying.org
200 Independence Avenue SW
Washington, DC 20201
Web site: http://www.stopbullying.gov
StopBullying.gov provides information from various
government agencies on what bullying is, what

cyberbullying is, who is at risk, and how you can prevent and respond to bullying.

STOP Cyberbullying
Wired Kids, Inc.
PMB 342 4401-A Connecticut Avenue NW
Washington, DC 20008
(201) 463-8663
Web site: http://www.stopcyberbullying.org
This organization is dedicated to showing children and
     educators how they can help prevent and take a
     stand against the practice of cyberbullying.

WEB SITES

Due to the changing nature of Internet links, Rosen Publishing has developed an online list of Web sites related to the subject of this book. This site is updated regularly. Please use this link to access the list:

http://www.rosenlinks.com/HELP/Safe

FOR FURTHER READING

Abram, Carolyn. *Facebook for Dummies*. Hoboken, NJ: Wiley, 2012.

Anthony, Michelle. *Little Girls Can Be Mean*. New York, NY: St. Martin's Griffin, 2010.

Claypoole, Ted. *Protecting Your Internet Identity.* Lanham, MD: Rowman & Littlefield Publishers, 2012.

Coloroso, Barbara. *The Bully, the Bullied, and the Bystander.* New York, NY: William Morrow Paperbacks, 2009.

Conifer, Dave. *EBully*. Seattle, WA: CreateSpace, 2010.

Conn, Kathleen. *Bullying and Harassment: A Legal Guide for Educators*. Alexandria, VA: Association for Supervision & Curriculum Development, 2004.

Criswell, Patti Kelley. *Stand Up for Yourself and Your Friends.* Middleton, WI: American Girl, 2009.

Dupre, Anne Proffitt. *The Unintended Costs of Free Speech in Public Schools*. Cambridge, MA: Harvard University Press, 2010.

Ellis, Deborah. *We Want You to Know: Kids Talk About Bullying*. Regina, SK, Canada: Coteau Books, 2011.

50 Cent. *Playground*. New York, NY: Razorbill, 2011.

Green, Susan. *Don't Pick On Me: Help for Kids to Stand Up and Deal with Bullies*. Oakland, CA: Instant Help, 2010.

Greenberg, Grant. *Facebook and Privacy: What You Need to Know to Keep Your Privacy Safe*. Seattle, WA: Amazon Digital Services, 2010.

Hinduja, Sameer. *Bullying Beyond the Schoolyard: Preventing and Responding to Cyberbullying*. Thousand Oaks, CA: Corwin Press, 2008.

Hunter, Nick. *Cyber Bullying*. Mankato, MN: Heinemann-Raintree, 2011.

Ivester, Matt. *LOL...OMG! What Every Student Needs to Know About Online Reputation Management, Digital Citizenship, and Cyberbullying*. Seattle, WA: CreateSpace, 2011.

Jacobs, Thomas. *Teen Cyberbullying Investigated*. Minneapolis, MN: Free Spirit Publishing, 2010.

Kowalski, Robin. *Cyberbullying: Bullying in the Digital Age*. Hoboken, NJ: Wiley-Blackwell, 2012.

Ludwig, Trudi, and Adam Gustavson. *Just Kidding*. Berkeley, CA: Tricycle Press, 2006.

MacEachern, Robyn. *Cyberbullying: Deal with It and Ctrl Alt Delete It*. Chapel Hill, NC: Lorimer Press, 2009.

Wiseman, Rosalind. *Queen Bees and Wannabes.* New York, NY: Three Rivers Press, 2009.

BIBLIOGRAPHY

Batteh-Freiha, Joy. "Boy Bullies vs. Girl Bullies: The Similarities and the Differences." Jacksonville.com, June 9, 2010. Retrieved June 10, 2012 (http://jacksonville.com/entertainment/2010-06-07/story/boy-bullies-vs-girl-bullies).

Bluestein, Greg, and Dorie Turner. "School Cyberbullying Victims Fight Back in Lawsuits." *Huffington Post*, April 26, 2012. Retrieved June 16, 2012 (http://www.huffingtonpost.com/2012/04/26/school-cyberbullying-vict_n_1457918.html).

Claudio, Cerullo. "Cyber Bullying Statistics." Teach Anti Bullying Inc. January 5, 2011. Retrieved June 15, 2012 (http://drclaudiocerullo.com/2011/01/05/cyber-bullying-statistics).

Copeland, Libby. "The Case of Karen Klein, Bullied Bus Monitor, Proves that Bullying Isn't Personal." Slate.com, June 22, 2012. Retrieved June 22, 2012 (http://www.slate.com/blogs/xx_factor/2012/06/22/karen_klein_bullied_bus_monitor_and_the_nature_of_middle_school_bullying_.html).

GirlsHealth.Gov. "Why Girls Bully." June 25, 2008. Retrieved June 22, 2012 (http://www.girlshealth.gov/bullying/whybully/).

Goldman, Russell. "Teens Indicted After Allegedly Taunting Girl Who Hanged Herself." ABC News, March 29, 2010. Retrieved June 19, 2012 (http://

abcnews.go.com/Technology/TheLaw/teens
-charged-bullying-mass-girl-kill/story?id
=10231357#.T_aIEM14xuF).

Hansen, Kevin A. "Seven Shocking Bully Regrets."
HuffingtonPost, June 6, 2012. Retrieved June 10,
2012 (http://www.huffingtonpost.com/kevin-a
-hansen/bullying_b_1617570.html).

Hoffman, Jan. "How Should Schools Handle
Cyberbullying?" *New York Times*, June 27, 2010.
Retrieved June 16, 2012 (http://www.nytimes
.com/2010/06/28/style/28bully.
html?pagewanted=all).

Leach, Jimmy. "Are Girls Worse Bullies Than Boys?"
Mortarboard blog, *Guardian*, March 8, 2006.
Retrieved June 20, 2012 (http://www.guardian
.co.uk/education/mortarboard/2006/mar/08
/aregirlsworsebulliesthanb).

Lee, Marie Myung-Ok. *Interview with My Bully: When I
Confronted My Bully About Racism*. Salon.com,
February 14, 2012. Retrieved July 1, 2012 (http://
www.salon.com/2012/02/14/interview_with_my
_bully_when_i_confronted_my_bully_about_racism/).

Lohnmann, Raychelle Cassada. "Teen Angst."
Psychology Today, June 30, 2011. Retrieved July 2,
2012 (http://www.psychologytoday.com/blog
/teen-angst/201107/cyberbully-protection).

Mishna, Faye, et al. "Cyber Bullying Behaviors Among
    Middle and High School Students."*American Journal
    of Orthopsychiatry*, July 2010. Retrieved July 1,
    2012 (http://www.ncbi.nlm.nih.gov/pubmed
    /20636942).

National Conference of State Legislatures.
    "Cyberbullying." 2012. Retrieved July 4, 2012
    (http://www.ncsl.org/issues-research/educ
    /cyberbullying.aspx).

Puresight. "Real Life Stories." Retrieved July 1, 2012
    (http://www.puresight.com/Real-Life-Stories
    /real-life-stories.html).

Sharma, Vijai P. "Psychological Profiles of Bullies
    and Victims." Mind Publications.com. Retrieved
    June 22, 2012 (http://www.mindpub.com
    /art192.htm).

Tan, Kevin. "Protecting Yourself from Cyberbullies."
    Scoga.org, July 12, 2012. Retrieved July 2, 2012
    (http://www.psychologytoday.com/blog
    /teen-angst/201107/cyberbully-protection).

Teach Today. "Dealing with Cyberbullying." Retrieved
    June 25, 2012 (http://www.teachtoday.eu/en
    /Teacher-advice/Cyberbullying.aspx).

TrueCare. "Cyberbullying Statistics You Should Know."
    TrueCare.com, January 11, 2011. Retrieved June 15,

2012 (http://www.truecare.com/blog/cyberbullying
/cyberbullying-statistics-you-should-know/).

Walsh, Ella. "How Bullies Pick Their Victims." KidSpot.
com.au. Retrieved June 12, 2012 (http://www
.kidspot.com.au/Preschool-Behaviour-How-bullies
-pick-their-victims+112+33+article.htm).

Watson, Angus. "Why I Used to Bully." *Telegraph*, June
7, 2004. Retrieved June 20, 2012 (http://www
.telegraph.co.uk/education/educationnews/3340735
/Why-I-used-to-be-a-bully.html).

ABOUT THE AUTHOR

Tracy Brown has written several books for young adults on a variety of topics. She lives in the Netherlands with her husband and two children.

PHOTO CREDITS

Cover © iStockphoto.com/Machineheadz; p. 5 F1online/Thinkstock; p. 8 1000 Words/Shutterstock.com; pp. 12, 23, 52–53, 58–59, 60–61, 65 © AP Images; p. 19 E. Dygas/Taxi/Getty Images; p. 24 Petrenko Andriy/Shutterstock.com; p. 26 Peter Cade/Iconica/Getty Images; p. 29 Hemera/Thinkstock; pp. 32–33 Digital Vision/Thinkstock; pp. 38–39 Dan Kitwood/Getty Images; pp. 40–41 Press Association/AP Images; p. 43 Stockbyte/Thinkstock; pp. 44–45 Mark Leffingwell/AFP/Getty Images; pp. 50–51 Image Source/Getty Images; pp. 1, 7, 11, 12, 13, 17, 20, 23, 28, 31, 36, 42, 46, 48, 57, 62 background pattern (telephones) © iStockphoto.com/Oksana Pasishnychenko; cover and interior telephone icons © iStockphoto.com/miniature.

Designer: Nicole Russo; Editor: Bethany Bryan; Photo Researcher: Marty Levick